THE CLARENDON BIOGRAPHIES

General Editors: C. L. MOWAT and M. R. PRICE

WILLIAM COBBETT

by

ASA BRIGGS

Professor of History, University of Sussex

OXFORD UNIVERSITY PRESS

1967

First published 1967

Reprinted in Canada 1969

FOR RUTH AND DANIEL

Printed in Canada by

T. H. BEST PRINTING COMPANY LIMITED

CONTENTS

LIST OF PLATES

1

PERSPECTIVES

WILLIAM COBBETT, the great radical leader of the early nineteenth century, was born in 1763 and died in 1835. One year before his death, he planned to write an autobiography called 'The Progress of a Ploughboy to a seat in Parliament, as exemplified in the History of the Life of William Cobbett, Member for Oldham'. The frontispiece to the autobiography would consist of two pictures—one of the young Cobbett dressed in a smock, driving away rooks from a cornfield, and the other of the old Cobbett standing in the House of Commons and addressing the Speaker.

This autobiography was never written, yet the idea of it reveals much about Cobbett. He was perpetually fascinated by his own experience and proud of it, and he wrote enough autobiographical fragments to make it possible to piece together the kind of book that he would probably have written. With no formal education —indeed, he always despised formal education—Cobbett had forcefully made his way ahead in the world and had left his distinctive mark upon it. By 1835 his name was more widely known in his country than that of most of his most distinguished and privileged contemporaries; and it was known in cottages as well as in country houses, in cities and villages, in North and South alike. William Hazlitt described him as a 'kind of fourth estate in the politics of the country', while the writer of his obituary in *The Times* explained that 'this self-taught peasant . . . . was, perhaps, in some respects a more extraordinary man than any other of his time'. His fame survived his death, and he continued to be remembered as much for the achievements of his life as for the sturdy and powerful writings which he left behind him. In the United States, where he spent eight formative years of his life from 1792 to 1800, a book about him was published in 1883 called *How to get on in the World, as Illustrated by the Life of William Cobbett.*

Yet Cobbett was no ordinary hero of self-help, the kind of man who adjusted himself to things as they were and preoccupied himself with achieving success. He never adjusted himself. Living in a period of revolutionary change, when old ideas and systems of society were being overturned, he resisted much that was happening. 'This *was* the happiest country in the world,' he exclaimed in 1830, 'it *was* the country of roast beef; it *was* distinguished above *all* other nations for the good food, good raiment and good morals, of its people; and it is now as much distinguished for the contrary of all of them.' His radicalism looked to the past, not to the future—to recovery rather than to transformation. As for his character, it was not quite as simple as he liked to believe. He was prejudiced as well as belligerent, and some of his prejudices were unpleasant and some silly. He knew how to tell a lie when it suited him, yet he always appeared supremely self-confident and tenacious. He had no subtlety, but he never lacked prudence. He misunderstood many people and many points of view—and he was forced on several occasions to change his mind both about people and issues—yet he had warm human sympathies which drew him to support the least well-off sections of the community, including men and women whose lives were as colourless as his was colourful. He spoke through the smoke and appealed to 'the weaver-boys of Lancashire' and their fellow-workers in Yorkshire, Derbyshire, and Nottingham, yet he was happiest in the fresh air of his own garden. Above all else, he prided himself on his independence. He never changed his prejudices, though he often changed his mind. At the last, he wrote simply in 1835:

If I have one wish more ardent than all other, it is this; that I enjoying my garden and few fields, may see England as great in the world, and her industrious, laborious, kind and virtuous people as happy as they were when I was born; and that I may at last have a few years of calm at the close of a long life of storms and of tempests.

There were to be no years of calm, but even if he had lived beyond 1835 it is doubtful whether there could have been. England at the time of Cobbett's death was on the eve of a period of even more fierce unrest than that which he had known, when the old ways of life were to disappear for ever. Industrial depression was to goad men into new lines of action. Whig and Tory governments alike were to carry measures of which Cobbett would have totally disapproved, and Chartists were to proclaim new versions of popular radicalism. Railways were increasingly to integrate the local communities of England which Cobbett had explored on horseback or by coach: new routines and new institutions were to establish themselves and be taken for granted.

In a sense, Cobbett was, in a phrase of G. D. H. Cole, 'the tribune of the transition', living through disturbed years when the shape of the future was blurred and indistinct. It was his lot in life to act at times as a national spokesman of discontent, at other times as a catalyst. He sympathized with and expressed many other people's grievances as well as his own: he also stirred them up. It is impossible, therefore, fully to separate out his private experience from the general experience of his age. The causes he took up can be clearly explained only in terms of the social and political history of his country. A frontispiece centred on a farmer's smock and the Speaker's mace would thus be quite inadequate for a modern biography of him: a place would have to be found also—in what would become an elaborate tapestry— for corn and coal, rights of man, war and depression, 'patriots' and 'radicals'. At the beginning of his life, England was an essentially agricultural society, enriched, more than Cobbett ever knew, by trade: at the end of it was a society in the throes of industrialization. At the beginning, the social system was based on rank, order, and degree—on men knowing their place in society: at the end, society was sharply divided into classes. At the beginning, the unreformed political system rested firmly on the power of property, while allowing scope for individual Members of Parliament to display independence of judgement and action: at the end, within a half-reformed political system, the new middle classes, but not the new working classes, had secured the right to vote.

So much changed in Cobbett's lifetime and so much else was about to change that, in order to defend the old, he had to become a radical to do so. 'We want nothing new,' was his constant cry, 'we want only what our forefathers enjoyed', yet the more vehemently he felt this, the more he was forced to employ new tactics which themselves marked a sharp break with the past. What started with prejudices ended with paradoxes. At almost every stage of his life Cobbett was caught up in politics of change, although he once wrote to a friend in 1793 telling God to preserve him from 'the political pest'. 'Let them fight and tear one anothers eyes out.' This was one piece of advice— and Cobbett loved to give advice—which he himself never followed. In consequence, his career was as turbulent as his times.

2

FOUNDATIONS

ALMOST everything that we know about Cobbett's early years derives from his own highly selective autobiographical fragments. The exception is the date of his birth—9 March 1763: Cobbett frequently mis-stated this date, giving the impression that he was three years younger than he was. He had three brothers, the exact age of whom he also forgot. Time clearly meant something very different in eighteenth-century England from what it does today, and Cobbett, whose father was a small farmer, who also kept an inn—appropriately called 'The Jolly Farmer'—was content to write, 'All that I can boast of in my birth is that I was born in Old England'.

Place of birth was more meaningful than time of birth. Cobbett was born in Farnham, Surrey, in a village set in the middle of hopfields—he called the spot 'the neatest in England, and I believe in the whole world'. Neither he nor his family knew much in the late 1760s and 1770s of 'the whole world', although news percolated through concerning the events of war across the Atlantic, where in 1776 the Americans proclaimed their independence. Cobbett's father sympathized with the Americans. In the course of time William Cobbett was to get to know the new United States at first hand—indeed to contribute to the making of American as well as English history. As a boy, however, his preoccupations were with English rural life—riding, hunting, visiting fairs, playing cricket. Most of his memories of boyhood concerned play rather than work. He could remember driving birds from fields, weeding, hoeing, ploughing, and gardening, but it was the holidays which stood out. He also remembered everybody being well fed. There was a golden glow over Cobbett's happy boyhood which in maturity influenced his interpretation not only of his own life but of English history.

School did not figure in these memoirs, and it was his father who taught him how to read and to write and to do simple arithmetic. Grammar was not his father's strong point, and, not surprisingly, given his independent temperament, William Cobbett became quite a specialist in grammar during his later life. He generalized, as usual, from his own early experience, and throughout his life expressed nothing but contempt for schools and for formal education, including that provided in what he called 'those dens of dunces called Colleges and Universities'. He felt that it had been an immense advantage to him that he had been spared a public education—'Heddukashion', he contemptuously called it: children should not be herded together in large numbers, as in 'jails, barracks and factories'. They should grow and develop naturally in their families under the personal care of their parents, learning good habits and preparing themselves in mind and in character for life as they would live it.

Given this view of self-education, it is not surprising that Cobbett picked out one incident in his childhood, which all his later biographers have been forced to pick out also. If his father taught him good habits—as much by practice as by precept— Cobbett himself discovered the joys of reading. At the age of fourteen, he set out on an excursion to Kew Gardens without saying a word to anyone and with only thirteen halfpennies in his pocket. On the way he spent his last threepence at Richmond on Jonathan Swift's *Tale of a Tub*, which he read avidly under a haystack. 'The book was so different from anything that I had ever read before,' he wrote later, 'that though I could not at all understand some of it, it delighted me beyond description.' It also produced 'a sort of birth of the intellect'. Perhaps, indeed, it did more than this: it fortified Cobbett's imagination and made him realize what an effective vehicle of the imagination a strong prose style can be. Other boys of fourteen have been fired by poetry: Cobbett, who was to be a master of prose satire himself, was fired by Swift.

The Kew adventure did not end with the buying of a book. Cobbett got a job for a time in the magnificent King's gardens

at Kew, gardens influenced by Chinese art, which were as skil-
fully designed to stimulate the imagination as any book. Even
more exciting, Cobbett caught a glimpse of the Prince of Wales,
later George IV, and his brothers: he was to publish a critical
history of the reign of George IV in 1830. Yet Kew was only a
brief episode—his father soon took him home—and in retrospect
it was set alongside another lasting teenage memory, that of a
visit to Portsmouth, where he tried, in vain, at the age of nine-
teen, to become a sailor. This time his imagination was stimulated
by the sight of the Grand Fleet riding at anchor off Spithead: he
was lost 'between astonishment and admiration' and dreamed of a
new life at sea, a life which later he was to judge 'the most toil-
some and perilous profession in the world'.

One thing was certain: Cobbett was not a conventional country
boy. He returned once more to the plough, but he was 'spoiled
for a farmer' and 'sighed for a sight of the world'. 'The little
island of Britain seemed too small a compass for me.' He was
obviously not going to follow in the footsteps of his grandfather
who had worked for the same master for forty years from
marriage to death, nor even in those of his father who was content
to acquire 'some little weight' in his own village. Young Cobbett
was big and strong—over six feet tall—and, with his ruddy
complexion and sturdy shoulders, looked like a farmer, yet he
was restless and ambitious. He lived in a society, however, where
the avenues of ambition were both limited and obscure, and it
took him many years to find himself.

At first, like so many other ambitious boys, he looked eagerly
towards London, and worked there for several months from 1783
to 1784 as a clerk to an attorney at Grays Inn. Characteristically,
he had gone up to London by stage coach on sudden impulse
instead of accompanying 'two or three lassses to Guildford Fair'
as he had planned, and once there he stayed. He was obviously
far less suited to be a clerk than he had been to be a farmer, and
he hated 'the gloomy recess' where he was called upon to work
from five in the morning until eight or nine at night. The ex-

perience was not wasted in that it cured him for life of writing 'saids' and 'so forths' and all similar 'counts of tautology'.

The law was not to be Cobbett's *forte*, although he was never for long able to keep clear of lawyers. Instead, in 1784, he enlisted for the Army. He had intended to join the Marines, but quickly found himself in the 54th Infantry Regiment. Fighting in America had ended in 1783, and for thirteen months he was kept in regimental barracks at Chatham. This too was not a happy period of his life. Many of his fellow recruits were young and raw, like him 'straight from the plough tail'. They were badly paid, harshly treated, and ill fed. 'The whole week's food was not a bit too much for one day.' Cobbett quite deliberately separated himself from his comrades and made the best use of his time. He was promoted to corporal, a sign that he impressed his officers more than they impressed him, but, more important, he used most of his leisure time 'not in the dissipations common to such a way of life, but in reading and study'. He subscribed to a circulating library, and read twice over most of the novels, plays, histories, and books of poems he could find there. Very systematically also he applied himself to grammar. 'The edge of my berth or that of the guard-bed,' he wrote later, 'was my seat to study in; my knapsack was my bookcase; a bit of board lying on my lap was my writing table.' As copyist to the Commandant of the garrison, he remained a clerk, although he was now a clerk in uniform, and, despite all the hardships of barrack life, he was proud of the worsted knot on his shoulder which displayed his rank and, more substantially, entitled him to an extra two-pence a day to augment his basic daily pay of sixpence.

After thirteen months, Cobbett's regiment at last set sail across the Atlantic from Gravesend for Nova Scotia. The voyage was pleasant, but Nova Scotia was a disappointment, as was New Brunswick where he soon moved. In a homely agricultural image Cobbett called Nova Scotia, New Brunswick and Canada 'the horns, the head, the neck, the shins, and the hoof of the ox', whereas the United States was 'the ribs, the sirloin, the kidneys, and the rest of the body'. Cobbett hated both the landscape and the climate, although he loved the great rivers and their creeks. He enjoyed skating, hunting, and fishing, and simply watching the life of the river change from season to season. He was fascinated also by local Canadian society. The exiled loyalist captains and colonels of the American War were eking out a precarious existence, and their titles sounded ironical. As a village boy born in a hierarchical society Cobbett 'had never thought of approaching a "Squire" without a most respectful bow; but, in this new world, though I was but a corporal, I often ordered a "Squire" to bring me a glass of grog, and even to take care of my knapsack'.

Cobbett stayed in this 'new world' for seven years from 1784 to 1791, and during this period learned a great deal not only about the limitations of Canadian captains and colonels but about the limitations of his own officers. He enjoyed being a soldier and throughout his later life claimed that he preferred soldiers as a class 'better than any other description of men', yet as always, he pursued his own private path, with vigour, determination, and single-mindedness of purpose. He worked hard and lived frugally, rising early in the morning—in summer at daylight, in winter at four o'clock—and being ready and alert before any of his comrades were out of bed. Not surprisingly, these qualities by themselves fitted him admirably for the post of Sergeant-Major to the Regiment, to which he was promoted over the heads of thirty sergeants. Before long he was—at least, in his own estimation—running the regiment. The officers were, he believed, 'in every respect except mere authority, my inferiors'. Not that, as a sergeant-major, he underestimated authority. While he came to despise his officers 'for their gross ignorance and their vanity' and to hate them for 'their drunkenness and rapacity'—he also despised the Adjutant for his ignorance of grammar—he was 'fully sensible of their power'. Indeed, the discipline of the regiment was in his hands, and he felt that everyone, in the last resort, depended upon him.

It was a curious but probably not a unique situation for a self-educated and proud young soldier with no qualifications of birth or influence. And, given Cobbett's tough independence of mind and very limited experience of the ways of the world, it was a difficult and potentially dangerous position. Cobbett's commanding officer, Major Edward Fitzgerald, was certainly not a fool, and both he and the Colonel of Cobbett's regiment thought sufficiently highly of Cobbett ultimately to recommend him for a commission. But by then Cobbett had discovered that the quarter-master of his regiment, 'who had the issuing of the men's provisions to them, kept about a fourth part of it to himself'. Cobbett was so upset by the scandal of this that he resolved to expose it publicly, and quietly came to the conclusion that in order to do this he would have to leave the Army once his regiment had returned to England. From 1787 to 1791 he began to collect materials for an exposure, collecting necessary extracts from regimental books and in the last few months winning the confidence of a corporal, William Bestland, who could serve as a witness. 'To work we went, and during a long winter, while the rest were boozing and snoring, we gutted no small part of the regimental books, rules and other dicuments.'

Cobbett's plot failed—and it was his first failure in life, and one of the most momentous of all his failures. His regiment returned to England in 1791, and Cobbett, refusing a commission, duly secured his discharge. In January 1792 he informed the Secretary of War about the circumstances of the case, and was surprised that he had to wait for ten days for a reply. A visit to the Secretary produced little satisfaction, and Cobbett was unsuccessful also in his efforts to persuade the Secretary to hold a court-martial of the quarter-master in London rather than in Portsmouth, where he feared intimidation of witnesses. Irritated by what he considered to be unwarrantable opposition and procrastination, Cobbett decided to write to the Prime Minister himself, William Pitt. Possibly as a result of this, the court-martial was transferred to London. Corporal Bestland, however, Cobbett's key witness, could not secure his discharge from the Army, and Cobbett also learned that the officers and sergeants of his old regiment was conspiring with each other to swear that

Cobbett had been a political trouble-maker. At this point, Cobbett sensed real danger. 'My head was filled,' he wrote later, 'with the corruptions and baseness in the army,' and 'I knew nothing at all about politics', yet even he realized that with the French Revolution in the background, he would probably be the one to suffer and not the quarter-master. Indeed, he might end up among the transported convicts in the recently founded penal colony in Botany Bay, Australia. He decided, therefore, on the prudent maxim that discretion is the better part of valour, not to appear at the court-martial, which he himself had asked for, and to get out of the country as quickly as possible. In March 1792, he set sail once again—this time across the Channel—for revolutionary France. The quarter-master and two other officers were duly acquitted in default of the appearance of their accuser.

There are bits and pieces of this story which do not completely fit together. What is certain, however, is that Cobbett's military experience, instead of disciplining him as he succeeded in disciplining his regiment, further unsettled him. Single-handed—or with the help of Corporal Bestland—he had tried to expose a small scandal which was merely a tiny part of a vast system of eighteenth-century perks and patronage. This system he did not understand, nor did he even try to understand it: eventually it was to become identified in his mind with general corruption, what he was to call 'The Thing'. Many of Cobbett's later ideas about government were related to this first decisive episode in his political education. He had been ignorant, too, when he began to search the Quarter-Master's accounts, of what was happening in England and Europe, and the French Revolution of 1789 had passed him by. On his own, therefore, in a period when some members of the Government were beginning to take very seriously the threat of general revolution, he had raised what were obviously complex questions of soldiers' rights. Certainly his political education was accelerated in 1791 and 1792. He admitted later that in the period between leaving Canada and setting sail for France he had read the radical Tom Paine's writings and had become interested in republicanism. Moreover, during this same short spell he was associated with the writing of a pamphlet *The Soldier's Friend* which bitterly attacked abuses in relation to soldiers' pay and was bound to be treated with suspicion by the Government. There was, however, a kind of innocence about Cobbett. He still knew little about England and less about France. He had got married in February 1792, and his trip to France had some of the characteristics of a honeymoon.

His trip lasted for only six months, 'the six happiest months of my life': his marriage was to last for the rest of his life, linking the various phases and periods together, 'through thick and thin'. He had first met his future wife—Ann Reid, the daughter of an artillery sergeant—in New Brunswick. Impressed both by her appearance—dark hair and good features—and her manners —modest, quiet, and industrious, a Cobbett recipe for women —he decided on marriage almost at sight. Fortunately, his feelings were reciprocated and her father approved. When she left New Brunswick for England before he did, he handed over to her for safe keeping his life savings, consisting of one hundred and fifty guineas. She carefully kept this money intact, and they were duly married in 1792 at the parish church in Woolwich. They were to have fourteen children, seven of whom survived. Cobbett was attracted by women, but he was cautious and virtuous, and if he had not become engaged to Ann Reid, he might have married a girl whom he met later in Canada. As it was, he had as definite views about marriage as about education, and expected from a wife (1) chastity, (2) sobriety, (3) industry, (4) frugality, (5) cleanliness, (6) knowledge of domestic affairs, (7) good temper, and (8) beauty—in that order. Happily, his own marriage was also a love match. 'One hair of her head,' he once wrote of his wife, 'is more dear to me than all the other women in the world.' His marriage, indeed, was one of the foundations on which the rest of his life was built.

William Cobbett, engraved by W. Ward after J. R. Smith.

COBBETT'S WEEKLY REGISTER.

VOL. 62.—No. 8.]   LONDON, SATURDAY, MAY 19, 1827.   [*Price 6d.*

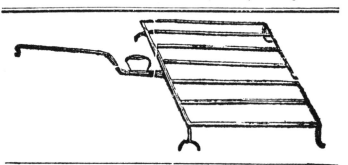

Top: Cobbett's birthplace at Farnham, Surrey.
Above: Title heading, *Cobbett's Weekly Register.*

Plate 2 from *The Life of William Cobbett*, written by himself, 29 September 1809.
A satirical biography by James Gillray (1757–1815), the leading political caricaturist
of his day. The illustration represents him 'flying from the embarrassments into
which he had run himself at home, and enlisting for a soldier'.

Plate 7 from *The Life of William Cobbett*, written by himself. 'He returns to England, and plots against the Government.'

3

EXILE AND PATRIOT

WHILE in France, the Cobbetts stayed in a quiet little northern village near St. Omer, where they met 'with civility, and even with hospitality'. Learning French was Cobbett's main occupation, as he had anticipated, and when in August 1793 curiosity led him towards Paris, the capital of revolution, he was so alarmed by the news of the deposition of King Louis XVI that he made another of those sudden flights which he was to make at many different points of his life. Completely switching his plans, he sailed with his wife for the United States, settled at Wilmington, about twenty miles from the American capital, Philadelphia, and made the most of his recent experience by teaching English to Frenchmen. There were more than enough Frenchmen in Wilmington and the surrounding neighbourhood to assure him of a good livelihood. Most of them were refugees from the French West Indies, where they were fleeing from Negro rebellion. Cobbett got on with them well and proved himself a good teacher. Indeed, he obviously imbibed many of their prejudices, for before long he had lost all sympathy with the French Revolution and had acquired—or perhaps fortified— a contempt for black people which stayed with him for the rest of his life. He never supported the emancipation of the slaves and thought that people who did were soft-hearted.

Cobbett arrived in the United States when the young country, independent for less than twenty years, was bitterly divided into two parties, or 'factions', as President Washington insisted on calling them. The Federalists had the support of the main urban economic interests—merchants, businessmen, and bankers: they also wished to remain on friendly terms with England. The Democrats were, as their names suggests, sympathetic to the principles of the French Revolution: they had strong support among landowners, frontiersmen, and town families with little or no property. Cobbett quickly became an active spokesman of anti-Democratic policies, not for reasons directly connected with America, but because of an unqualified English 'patriotism'. Behaving more like a soldier than a civilian, he was driven to fury when he heard Americans attacking his native country or supporting France instead. 'Who will say that an Englishman ought not to despise all nations in the world?' he asked belligerently in order to answer—'for my part I do and that most heartily.' Not surprisingly, he never became an American citizen —although immediately after arriving in Wilmington he had written to Jefferson, the great American democrat (democrat with a small and a large D), telling him that he was 'ambitious to become the citizen of a free state'. This ambition soon disappeared, although he made the fullest possible use of living in a free state—making money, acquiring influence, and, above all, spreading propaganda.

Teaching English was simply the first step, perpetuated though it was in Cobbett's first highly successful book, a grammar book, *Le Tuteur Anglais*. In January 1794 he moved to Philadelphia and discovered his true vocation—that of a political pamphleteer. The arrival of the great English dissenting minister, Dr. Joseph Priestley, one of the most remarkable men of his age, gave Cobbett his initial opportunity. Priestley, philosopher, scientist, and writer, had been forced to leave England because of his liberal political views. A Birmingham mob had destroyed his house, and throughout the country English opponents of the French Revolution were pointing him out as a dangerous 'cosmopolitan' who put his principles before his country. Naturally he was given a warm welcome in the United States, and this Cobbett resented, along with remarks Priestley made about England. In a state of great excitement Cobbett wrote a pamphlet *Observations on the Emigration of Joseph Priestley* attacking both Priestley's views and his reputation. When Matthew Carey, one of the two leading publishers in Philadelphia, refused to publish it (thereafter Cobbett always insisted on calling him 'O'Carey' and treating him as an Irish enemy), Cobbett took it to Carey's rival Thomas Bradford, who agreed to publish it only as an anonymous pamphlet with no publisher's name on the title page.

The pamphlet was the first of many, and understandably, like those which followed, it received warm acclamation from England, where it was reprinted. Pitt needed a vigorous anti-revolutionary press, and Cobbett obliged him without invitation or pressure. Yet in America also Cobbett won widespread support in conservative circles—after all, the country had only just ceased to be a collection of British Colonies—although he seems characteristically to have welcomed this support less than the vituperation of the American Democrats. He quickly proved himself to be a fearless controversialist, choosing the name Peter Porcupine as the most apt pseudonym to describe himself. The titles of his first pamphlets were almost as memorable as his pseudonym—*A Bone to Gnaw for the Democrats* and *A Kick for a Bite*. The latter provoked a reply called *A Rub from Snub*, and thereafter Cobbett got as much experience of political warfare as even he wished. He embroiled himself in a number of purely personal animosities, and quarrelled, into the bargain, with Bradford and his son. In 1796 he became his own publisher and bookseller. When he opened his bookshop he defied 'the mob' by crowding into the window 'all the portraits I had in my possession of kings, queens, princes and nobles ... several of the Bishops and Judges: the most famous Admirals: and in short every picture I thought likely to excite rage in the enemies of Great Britain'.

This flamboyant, foolhardly guesture gained him publicity, yet in themselves his pamphlets were sufficiently militant to ensure his success. Indeed, these early pamphlets bear many of the marks of his later style, while one innovation was to point to his most significant success later. Realizing that events were moving so fast that pamphlets might as well become periodicals and welcoming enthusiastically the prospect of a regular encounter with a reading public that would begin to get to know him, he started a new monthly journal, *The Political Censor,* designed to review the political transactions of the previous month. 'Here then, begins a *bellum eternum* between the fabricating *Quid-Nuncs* and me.' It was soon talked about everywhere, and Cobbett loved the limelight:

> When I had the honour to serve King George, I was elated enough at the putting on of my worsted shoulder knot, and afterwards, my silver-laced coat; what must my feelings be then, upon seeing half a dozen authors, or *Doctors,* or the devil knows what, writing about me at one time, and ten times that number of printers, bookbinders, and booksellers, bustling, running and flying about in all directions, to announce my fame to the impatient public? What must I feel upon seeing the newspapers filled from top to bottom, and the windows and corners of the houses placarded with a . . . . : a *Pill for Peter Porcupine, Peter Porcupine Detected,* a *Roaster for Peter Porcupine,* a *History of Peter Porcupine,* a *Picture of Peter Porcupine*? The public will certainly excuse me, if after all this, I should begin to think myself a person of some importance.

Cobbett followed up *The Political Censor* with a daily news sheet, *Porcupine's Gazette,* which first appeared in March 1797. Its appearance coincided with President Washington's retirement and his replacement by Adams. Washington did not subscribe to the *Gazette,* but considered doing so. At the height of its circulation, it sold over three thousand copies each day.

The note of self-praise with which Cobbett chronicled his own contribution to American life somewhat mars the general impression. Nor did he ever lose this egotistical note. Cobbett openly referred everything in the world to himself, so that his egotism was always, as Hazlitt wrote, 'naked' and 'above board'. This does not mean, however, that it is always easy to take. In later life, in 1829, he was to sum up his achievement with limitless self-confidence: 'I became in America, beginning with the year

1794, a most industrious, indefatigable, zealous and, I may add, able defender of the rights of England.' At the time, indeed, he seemed so forceful a defender of British rights that the Democrats believed that he had been bribed by the British Government. In the words of a poem of 1797, *The Royal Cockneys in America*, Cobbett was:

> *Porcupine Peter*
> *The Democrat-eater*
> *Transported by Pitt at the charge of the nation*
> *To preach to the demos a new revelation.*

To deal with this kind of criticism, which rested on a complete misunderstanding of Cobbett's temperament, Cobbett produced an extremely readable and convincing self-portrait, *The Life and Adventures of Peter Porcupine*. He remained more gentle to himself, however, than to the people whom he so bitterly attacked. Having disposed of Priestley, about whom he was almost completely ignorant, he turned his attention to Tom Paine, the radical leader, about whom he knew little, and wrote a scurrilous *Life*, which was a great success in Pitt's England. One of his American critics compared Cobbett at this time to a 'headstrong horse, that runs off with his rider', dashing 'through mud and mire, making the dirt fly in all directions.'

Inevitably such exuberant activities were bound, even in a free country, to lead to litigation. Before that, however, they were to lead to a remarkable offer on the part of the French to win him over to their side as a journalist. No less a person than Talleyrand approached him, to be quickly snubbed when he asked Cobbett if he had been educated at Oxford or Cambridge. The litigation began in 1797, when the Spanish ambassador, nicknamed by Cobbett 'Don Sans-Culotta de Carmagnola', and described by him as the recently arrived representative of the '*magnanimous ally of the murderers of Louis XVI*', brought an action against him for libel. A Pennsylvania grand jury threw out the bill against Cobbett by ten votes to nine, but the Chief Justice, Thomas M'Kean, Democratic politician as well as judge, headed the list of witnesses against him. A new Cobbett pamphlet on M'Kean called *The Democratic Judge* was hardly evidence of Cobbett's habitual prudence when crisis loomed, nor did M'Kean welcome quite unfair comparisons with the notorious Judge Jefferys or quite untrue allegations that the English Press was more free than that in the United States. Cobbett was obviously now beginning to write for an English audience first and an American audience second. The decisive litigation came in 1799, two years after Cobbett had attacked a well-known physician, Dr. Benjamin Rush, for a 'quack' treatment of yellow fever. He was not the only pamphleteer to do this, but perhaps he was particularly devastating in his blunt and effective satire.

Between 1797 and 1799, when the Rush libel case was heard in Philadelphia, M'Kean had become governor of Pennsylvania and Cobbett had made a desperate attempt to encourage the Americans to go to war against the French. He published *The Complete Soldiers' Pocket Companion* during this period and headed a regular column of his Gazette 'Military Intelligence'. He also tried to get Americans to wear a black cockade in opposition to the tricolour, and warned them luridly of an imminent French invasion. All this from an Englishman was going too far, although many members of the Federal Party sympathized with what he was saying. Unfortunately for him, war fever abated with the yellow fever, which Rush had tried hopelessly to treat; President Adams showed that he believed America could live peacefully with France; and Cobbett, dangerously embroiled in local politics, had to suspend publication of *Porcupine's Gazette* and to flee from Philadelphia to New York. When the Rush case came before the Court, the verdict went against him. Once again he was *in absentia,* and the plaintiff was awarded the large sum of five thousand dollars.

Cobbett believed that he was being 'mulcted in this shameful manner' not for his views on the proper treatment of yellow fever but for his politics. Yet with his finances in confusion—not for the last time—he spent his final weeks in the United States producing a vitriolic fortnightly paper called *The Rushlight,* wholly devoted to the follies and crimes of Dr. Rush. On 1 June 1799 he set sail for England with his wife and the first of their two children who had been born there (two had died): as one opposition poet put it,

> *He took his leave from Sandy Hook*
> *And parted with a surly look*
> *That all observed and few mistook.*

On setting sail, Cobbett left behind in the New York newspapers what he called his 'farewell advertisement' to the American people. He asked for peace and happiness for his friends, whom he rightly said were numerous, kind, sincere, and faithful, and advised his enemies that he could wish them no 'severer scourge than that which they are preparing for themselves and their country'. 'With this,' he went on, 'I depart for my native land, where neither the moth of *Democracy,* nor the rust of *Federalism* doth corrupt, and where thieves do not, with impunity, break through and steal five thousand dollars at a time.'

4

CITIZEN AND CRITIC

COBBETT returned to England with invaluable experience as a tough and hard-hitting journalist and with the reputation of a patriot. His American pamphlets had been widely read and discussed in England, and he had many English correspondents as well as a good agent, John Wright, the Anti-Jacobin bookseller. It was scarcely surprising that on his return he had interviews first with William Windham, Secretary at War in Pitt's Government, and later with George Canning and Pitt himself. Although he claimed that his 'first wish' was 'to merit the commendations of men distinguished for their wisdom and loyalty', he refused a flattering invitation to edit a Government-backed daily paper, either the *True Briton* or the *Sun*, with all the money and influence that such a post would have brought with it, on the grounds that he would thereby lose his independence. A few months before leaving America he had told a friendly fellow-journalist, 'I have always been *independent* and I must always remain so ... life is not life with me, unless I am master, sole master, of my thoughts and actions.' He soon realized that refusing Pitt's invitation not only barred him entry to Government circles, but made Government suspicious of him. Fortunately Windham remained a true friend. Unlike Cobbett, he was a gentleman by birth and a friend of scholars and men of letters by inclination: he was also thoughtful and generous. Like Cobbett, he preferred the old ways to the new and, moving in the shadow of Edmund Burke, he was a fierce enemy of the French Revolution.

As a citizen of his own country, Cobbett had as much to learn about England as he had to learn about America when he first had gone to the United States in 1793. Even the landscape seemed strange: 'the trees, the hedges, the parks and woods seemed so small ... The Thames was but a creek.' As for Farnham, the hill near the town had dwindled from a mountain to a mound. Social gradations, however, had changed less than the contours of the landscape, except that far more people called themselves 'squire' than Cobbett thought had the right to do so. Cobbett had many invitations to dine out and for the first time met large numbers of his own countrymen. He was not flattered. 'The distinctions of rank, birth and wealth all became nothing in my eyes ... and I resolved never to bend before them.'

The first thing to do was to earn a living. Cobbett had a low opinion of the ability of those journalists who in broad terms supported the cause of the Government, except for William Gifford, the editor of *The Anti Jacobin,* who wanted a quiet and comfortable life, and John Reeves, a shrewd lawyer, who had been chairman of the ultra-conservative Association for the Preservation of Liberty and Property against Republicans and Levellers, founded in 1792, when most popular societies preached opposite principles. Reeves and Gifford made it clear to Cobbett that they had few illusions about politics, but it took time for Cobbett to find out for himself. He succeeded in October 1800 in founding a daily paper, *The Porcupine,* to support the Government—with Rush still in mind, it refused all advertisements of patent medicines—but it was not a financial success and was soon sold in November 1801 and merged in the *True Briton,* one of the two papers which had been 'offered' to Cobbett on his arrival back home. It was Windham who helped Cobbett financially to launch his next venture—on the strict written understanding that Cobbett was to be as free as if he had started it himself. The result was the *Political Register* which was to be Cobbett's public voice for the rest of his life. Others wrote in the paper, but it was Cobbett who controlled policy and set the tone. It was, indeed, a kind of extension of himself, and in its changes of viewpoint reflected faithfully the changes of his own mind.

The first number appeared on 16 January 1802, attacking France as bitterly as the French Revolution and firmly criticizing the Government for having sought peace with France at Amiens in the autumn of 1801. The timing was fortunate—Pitt's Government had given way in 1801 to that of his friend, Henry Addington, later Viscount Sidmouth, a careful man of conventional opinions and inferior abilities, once described by Canning as 'Britain's guardian gander': the reason for the change was not policy towards France but King George III's veto on Catholic emancipation, which Pitt wanted to raise in the cabinet after the passing of the Act of Union with Ireland. Cobbett agreed with George III on this issue—Windham was with Pitt—although he was completely to change his mind later. More important at the time, he was able to launch his paper in opposition to the Government rather than on its side, for when after taking office Addington sought to make peace with France, his tactics were criticized not only by Cobbett, but by a group of Pitt's former supporters, among them those with the most unrelenting anti-Jacobin opinions. Cobbett might have been back in America again. He could be both patriot and critic at the same time. He characteristically refused to illuminate his house in Pall Mall on two occasions—first when the Peace of Amiens was announced and second when it was ratified in March 1802. On the first occasion all his windows were broken and the door forced: clearly the London 'mob' was less awed by him than the mob of Philadelphia. On the second occasion, it took a troop of horse-guards to disperse the crowd, many of whom were government clerks, who received no sympathy from Cobbett when they were arrested.

In the meantime, Cobbett was consolidating his other business activities just as he had done in America. In association with John Morgan, an American bookseller whom he had first met in Philadelphia, he published twelve volumes of *The Works of Peter Porcupine*. The Prince of Wales headed the subscription list for this publication. Cobbett also published *Letters to Hawkesbury* (later Lord Liverpool) *and Addington,* and learnt with pride in 1803, that Windham had told the House of Commons that he 'merited a statue of gold' for his work across the Atlantic.

Yet successful as many of these ventures were, particularly the *Political Register,* Cobbett was not at ease in his own country. He joined with Windham in successfully opposing a Bill in Parliament to suppress bull-baiting—one side, the 'manly sports side', of 'old England'—defended the slave trade against Wilberforce, whom he detested as repressive and sanctimonious, the biggest enemy of England's 'old free manners', and began to brood on public finance, particularly on the spread of paper money and the accumulation of the national debt. It was in relation to the last of these issues that Cobbett was to make his first turn towards 'radicalism'. He soon came to believe that one of the things most wrong with Britain was the war-time substitution of worthless paper for valuable gold. The Government was borrowing heavily to finance the war, and holders of government funds—a small minority, among whom there were many speculators—were receiving dividends which were paid for either out of taxation, levied on all, including the very poor, or were drawn from further borrowing. What was wrong with England was the City of London and 'the swarm of locusts who, without stirring ten miles from the capital, devour three-fourths of the produce of the whole land'.

Such a sturdy, simplified view of public finance gave ample opportunity for Cobbett to display most of his prejudices, including the unpleasant ones—in this case, dislike of the Jews. Much that he said about financial parasites has been repeated by right-wing critics of orthodox finance ever since. At the same time, Cobbett was genuinely and deeply concerned about the plight of ordinary people, who did not know where they stood when the value of money fluctuated and were forced to pay heavy indirect taxes to keep 'the system' going. He was also particularly upset by the fact that landlords, knowing that the value of money was falling, were unwilling to grant long leases to their tenant farmers, and tried to drive hard bargains, as prices rose, whenever leases were renewed. Moreover, the farm labourer never received more than enough to maintain himself and his family, and was often forced back on poor law assistance from the parish. In all these ways currency questions directed Cobbett's attention to 'the condition of England question', to an analysis or rather a series of related pictures of what was happening to English society. Strangely enough, he was converted to his role as a critic of the system partly at least by reading Tom Paine's *The Decline and Fall of the English System of Finance* (1796): thereafter Paine's reputation began to rise in his mind until he felt something like guilt—for the only time in his life—for what he had previously written about him. 'I saw the whole matter in its true light,' he wrote later in his *Paper Against Gold* (1815) about the effect of reading Paine, 'and neither pamphleteers nor speech-makers were, after that, able to raise a momentary puzzle in my mind.'

It took some time for Cobbett to relate his views about the financial system to his views about government and to draw the conclusion that statesmen had become 'subservient' to the views of 'money-lenders'. He continued throughout 1803 and 1804 to support the war as passionately as ever, noting, however, that after Pitt had returned to office in May 1804 his closest political friends, including Windham, were not included in the new Government. In his first *Letter to Pitt*, therefore, written in September 1804 and ominously sub-titled 'On the Causes of the Decline of Great Britain', he admitted that he had ceased to be Pitt's 'eulogist' and had become his 'assailant'. He had good words for Charles James Fox, Pitt's rival, while being at great pains—perhaps too great pains—to insist on his own consistency. It had always been and always would be his purpose, he wrote, 'to check the spirit and oppose the progress of levelling innovation, whether proceeding from clubs of jocabins, companies of traders, synagogues of saints, or boards of the government'. The list was comprehensive. He also had always been resolute, he added, in his advocacy of 'long tried principles' and sincere in his 'affection for ancient families and ancient establishments'.

Cobbett could move naturally towards a radical position between 1804 and 1807 without being in any doubt himself about his own consistency. There were four reasons for this. First, he could persuade himself—and he was not alone in doing so—that radical action meant nothing new: it was needed simply to *restore* the old constitution of England. His position on this question drew near to that of Sir Francis Burdett, head of a very old family, who was losing confidence in the Whigs while Cobbett was losing confidence in the Tories. It was only necessary 'to recur to the principles handed down by our forefathers' to put the country on its feet again. Second, he could argue that the abdication from government of what another radical, Joseph Hume was to call 'the natural magistracy', men who inherited influence, left the question of national leadership open. Where could England look if those who had been born to lead failed to lead? 'If there had been any great body of the nobility and gentry, starting forward for a reform of the system, the spirit of the country would have been very different, but we saw no such body.' Disraeli was to take up this argument with subtlety later in the century: to Cobbett it was a matter of plain common sense.

Third, because of the course of political events between 1804 and 1807, Cobbett, again like Burdett, could dismiss both Whigs and Tories as 'factions', 'ins', and 'outs', who between them perpetuated a political 'system' which was as adverse to the popular interest as the financial system. The main events which made possible this explanation were the death of Pitt in 1805—Cobbett refused to lament it—and the return to power in 1806 of the so called 'Ministry of All the Talents', which included Fox as Foreign Secretary and Windham as Secretary of State for War and the Colonies, along with old faces like Sidmouth and Grenville. Cobbett demanded a complete change of policy from the new administration and failed to get it. There were no big changes either in financial policy or in foreign policy. Pensions and sinecures and nepotism and all the abuses of government that Cobbett wanted to sweep away were all retained. Even Windham, with whom Cobbett remained on good personal terms after he had begun to attack everyone else, particularly Grenville and his family, failed to do anything to pursue 'A Plan for the Forming of an Efficient and Permanent Army' which Cobbett prepared for him.

Before long, Cobbett ceased to be a critic of the Ministry, became a genuine radical, and after 1806 began to demand large-scale parliamentary reform. The climax came at the Westminster election of 1807 when he told the electors 'to reject, with equal scorn, the appellation of *Foxite* (Fox also had died—soon after Pitt—in 1806), of *Pittite,* of *Whig*, or of *Tory*: that you may in the exercise of your elective rights, be influenced by *principles* and not by *names;* and that your conduct by becoming an example to electors in general, or a *timely indication to the elected* may lead to a constitutional reform of the gross abuses that exist'.

Fourth, events in Cobbett's own life encouraged the shift. In 1805 he had bought a house in the country near Botley in Hampshire, five miles from Southampton, far from 'the accursed smoke' of 'the great Wen' of London. There was an inevitable tension between the life of the country man and the life of the London journalist. With other men, the tension might have led to escape: with Cobbett, it led to a closer study of social contradictions. Why was London, 'the great Wen', so noisy and so nasty, and Hampshire, so quiet on the surface, yet so full of poverty and discontent? What was the meaning of the Hampshire enclosures of common land? In 1791 Cobbett had attacked malpractices in his own regiment without realizing he was attacking a system. Was it not clear now—in the light both of national politics and of his own private experience—that there was a national system —financial *and* political, each side supporting the other—which prevented people from being both happy and free, as they once had been? Cobbett's ideal of happiness had not changed as he grew older: indeed, life on his Botley 'estate' realized his ideal more fully than any life he had previously enjoyed. There were melons as well as primroses, a garden as well as a farm, and in this beautiful setting his family was growing in size and in interest as he believed all families should. What were the barriers to such happiness and freedom for everyone? The attempt to answer this question turned Cobbett not only into a radical but into a democrat.

In the meantime, however, it sharpened his dislike of men like William Wilberforce, who in Cobbett's opinion, forced 'the common people'—Cobbett used the term—to submit to new codes of behaviour which were in flat opposition to the old ways of life. 'On the selfishness of the common people, particularly the labouring part of them, the Pitt system of finance and taxation has, directly at least, no hold, and, therefore, it required the aid of the system of effeminacy which includes the suppression of mirth as well as of hardy exercises and indeed of everything that tends to produce relaxations from labour and a communication of ideas of independence among the common people.' Cobbett was unyielding in this attack on Evangelicalism as represented by Wilberforce and the 'Saints'. He also condemned Methodism and all other forms of latter-day Puritanism which were designed, in his view, to tame 'fierce manners'—and that is why Cobbett talked about 'effeminacy'—and to keep people quiet. 'Public education', which even his own friends were advocating, seemed to him to have the same end. 'Render the whole nation effeminate; suffer no relxation from labour or from care, shut all the paupers up in workhouses, and those that are not shut up, work in gangs each with its own driver; this do, and it is evident that you will have no internal commotion; it is evident that you will hold the people in complete subjection to your will.'

The importance of passages of this kind (in the *Political Register* for 10 August 1805) can scarcely be exaggerated. Cobbett was prepared for internal commotion: it was other people wanting to keep the nation quiet which seemed to him to be a wicked conspiracy. Already London wits had discovered that you could make an anagram 'FRANTIC DISTURBER' out of Francis Burdett's name. Cobbett, much more powerful potentially than Burdett ever could be, because he sprang from the common people and knew the right tone of address to win them over, began to incur the searching scrutiny of Government. Attempts were made to discredit him—the story of the court-martial, for example, was conveniently raked up—and new anti-Cobbett periodicals were launched. And when the Ministry of All the Talents was replaced, first by a Portland and then by a Spencer Percival administration, Cobbett was in serious danger, for, above all else, neither the aged Portland nor the fussy Spencer Percival could stand the thought of a nation-wide popular radical agitation.

Plate 8 from *The Life of William Cobbett*, written by himself. 'The denouement of this eventful history.'

Wm Cobbett

The author of the *Political Register*. From Fraser's Magazine, October 1835.

There is but one man
in the Country who can
extricate it from difficulties
why dont you send *Him* to Parliament".

Cobbett's lecture, by the political caricaturist H.B.

Common Ground (1951) Ltd.

Cobbett's death was commemorated by his friends with a bronze medallion, the front shows his profile as he appeared in later life. The other picture shows the reverse side of the same medallion with emblems—the pen and the plough— symbolizing his life.

5

THE MAKING OF A RADICAL

THE open clash with the Government was not to come until 1810. In the meantime, Cobbett had his first direct experience of parliamentary elections. In 1806 there was a by-election in the borough of Honiton in Devonshire, and Cobbett in the pages of the *Register* appealed for a high-minded and independent patriot to come forward and stand. If no one came forward, he added, he would stand himself. In fact, there was a volunteer—Lord Cochrane, son of the ninth Earl of Dundonald, a radical sea captain with a distinguished but chequered naval career ahead of him. Cochrane fought the seat on the strict understanding that he would not bribe the electors, and not surprisingly lost. Having lost, however, he offered everyone who had voted for him ten pounds ten shillings. Only four months later, Cochrane won the next election at Honiton.

Whatever the moral of this tale, it was the experience of Honiton which made Cobbett a convinced advocate of parliamentary reform, about which he had previously been either hostile or sceptical. As usual, he wrote about his discovery of rotten boroughs as if no one had ever thought them rotten before. How could people tolerate such 'a shocking abuse'? This was almost the last blow to Cobbett's innocence about the English political system, which ten years before he had held up to the Americans as a model. At the famous Westminster elections of 1806 and 1807, famous because they forced Westminster to the forefront of radical politics, Cobbett began to use the phrase 'We, the people'. In 1808 he had moved so far away from his original position that he could offer support to the popular radical 'Orator' Hunt and even boast about getting in a little 'democratical and Jacobinical talk' himself at a county meeting of electors in Hampshire. By this time, indeed, he had had enough experience of public speaking to know how to handle crowds as well as how to handle words. He had a good, loud voice and a commanding presence, and he refused to be put down. He recognized, however, that the power of an independent Press was more generally effective than the most eloquent platform address, and he devoted much of his time in 1807 and 1808 to attacking the 'bought press' which through thick and thin supported the Government. 'The press, which has been called the Palladium of free men . . . has, like many other things in our political state, been so completely perverted, as to be one of the chief means, by which . . . the freedom which an honest and loyal man ought to enjoy, has been nearly extinguished among us.'

The combination of politician and journalist was just what Government feared and also what men like Windham, remaining Tory in their views, found most distasteful; 'wicked and mischievous' Windham called his writings in 1809. Cobbett, however, believed in what he called 'enlightening' the people, *all* the people, rich and poor. In addition to the *Political Register*, which yielded him a steady income, he had begun in 1804 an enterprise called *Cobbett's Parliamentary Debates* which recorded *verbatim* proceedings in Parliament. The enterprise was sold to Hansard in 1812, the birth year of what was to become a great national institution. He also published *Cobbett's Parliamentary History of England*, which purported to tell the truth about everything that had happened in politics since 1066, and supervised a still invaluable compilation, *Cobbett's Complete Collection of State Trials*, started in 1809, and sold, like the *Debates*, to a new proprietor in 1812.

Before he himself got involved in yet another trial—for this was the form Cobbett's clash with Government was to take— he had changed his views on one important political question and strengthened his views on a second. First, he accepted the need for Catholic Emancipation, while rightly insisting that it would provide no complete solution for Ireland's complex problems. Second, he reiterated his support for the war against

France, and in 1807 and 1808 fiercely attacked those of his fellow-countrymen—and they were an increasing number—who wanted to make peace on the grounds that the war was damaging Britain's trade. His distaste for industry and for 'middle-class' industrialists, who were beginning to use the term 'middle-class' at this time to express their collective interest, was at least as strong as his love of the land. 'Spinning-Jenny Baronets'—and he had in mind the first Sir Robert Peel—were the worst of the bunch of 'mere buyers and sellers'. Cobbett's preference for agriculture against industry and his dislike of the new men of power in the North of England directed his growing radicalism into working-class channels. He began to sympathize with the 'victims of industry' as well as with the victims of enclosure. The sympathies were to broaden out much farther—and to deepen—after 1812.

The trial, however, related once again to the Army. In June 1809 Cobbett read the following paragraph in the *Courier*, one of the Government newspapers:

The mutiny among the local militia which broke out at Ely was fortunately suppressed on Wednesday by the arrival of four squadrons of the German Legion Cavalry from Bury, under the command of General Auckland. Five of the ringleaders were tried by a court-martial, and sentenced to receive five hundred lashes each, part of which punishment they received on Wednesday, and a part was remitted. A stoppage for their knapsacks was the ground of complaint that excited this mutinous spirit, which occasioned the men to surround their officers, and demand what they deemed their arrears. The first division of the German Legion halted yesterday at Newmarket on their return to Bury.

This paragraph infuriated Cobbett. He had tried to restrain his criticisms of the Government somewhat in 1808 and 1809, on grounds of prudence, but this paragraph touched such chords of his own experience that he, the Soldier's Friend, could not be silent—a legitimate complaint; the flogging of 'free-born Englishmen'; the use of German troops. Could Napoleon have done worse? Cobbett devoted more than one paragraph in the *Register* to the subject, but these angry, challenging *staccato* words stood out:

> *Five hundred lashes each!* Aye, that is right! Flog them! Flog! Flog! Flog! They deserve a flogging at every meal time. Lash them daily! Lash them daily! What! Shall the rascals dare to *mutiny*? And that, too, when the German Legion is so near at hand? Lash them! Lash them! Lash them! They deserve it, Oh, yes! They merit a double-tailed cat! Base dogs! What! mutiny for the price of a knapsack? Lash them! Flog them! Base Rascals!

On reading this passage, the Attorney-General filed an information against Cobbett for sedition, but thereafter the Government moved slowly, perhaps hoping to gag Cobbett without bringing him to trial. It was not until June 1810 that his case was brought before the Lord Chief Justice, Baron Ellenborough, a stern judge well used to dealing with political cases. Cobbett, who had made many preparations to set his private affairs in order before the trial was announced, unwisely decided—with far too much self-confidence—to conduct his own defence. The jury took only five minutes to find him guilty, but sentence was deferred.

In the interval between judgement and sentence, official and unofficial attempts were made to gag Cobbett for good by inducing him to abandon journalism and politics. Cobbett very nearly yielded: indeed, he wrote a *Farewell* article to his readers which was all ready for print. It included the final and terrible words, 'I never will again, upon any account, indite, publish, write or contribute towards any newspaper, or other publication of that nature, so long as I live.' The article was never published, for Cobbett changed his mind. According to his agent, John Wright, who talked to people who were in the know, the Government was not willing to drop the sentence in return for a surrender. Cobbett clearly could not yield without guarantees, however momentarily attractive the thought of a quiet life at Botley with his family might be. On 5 July he was called up for judgement and four days later heard the worst. His printer, Hansard, received three months imprisonment and his publishers two months each. He himself was sentenced to two years imprisonment and moved at once to Newgate gaol.

It was a crushing sentence, but it did not crush Cobbett. He lied later in denying that he had ever written a farewell article, but once having decided not to yield, his feeling of being right all along was fortified. 'Be you good children,' he wrote to his eldest boy, 'and we shall all have ample revenge.' He could buy many privileges for himself at Newgate—for the well-off, prisons were essentially detention centres in 1810—and Cobbett received very generous financial help from Sir Francis Burdett, who had himself in a *cause célèbre* been imprisoned in the Tower of London earlier in the same year. While in prison, Cobbett could continue to conduct the affairs of his farm, to see his wife, to receive his children, and to entertain his friends. More remarkable still, he could continue to edit the *Political Register*. After protracted wrangles about finance, for his affairs were not in a good state, he dismissed his old colleague John Wright, the man who had warned him about Government duplicity, and set to work himself. Indeed, from July 1800 to June 1811 the *Register* actually appeared twice a week instead of once. Wright spent a good deal of time and effort attacking Cobbett's reputation, but the attacks did Cobbett no harm. Instead, he was visited in prison 'by persons whom I had never seen before, from *one hundred and ninety-seven cities and towns of England, Scotland and Ireland*, the greatest part of whom came to me as the deputees of some society, club or circle of people in their respective spheres of residence'. Whatever else the Government had done, it had not gagged Cobbett, nor had it weakened his strength or resolution. While he was in gaol, Cobbett wrote, 'I was never ill for a single moment, I never had even a headache, and I felt myself as strong as at any period of my life.'

It was in Newgate that Cobbett wrote his 'Paper Against Gold' in which he put together all his thoughts on the currency in the light of the official report of the so-called Bullion Committee which appeared in September 1810. Reviewing the effects of the increased issue of paper money since 1797, when the Government had first allowed the Bank of England to make its payments in paper rather than in gold, the Committee concluded that there had been currency depreciation and that a law ought to be passed resuming gold payments as soon as possible. The Government refused to accept the report in the middle of the war against Napoleon—it would have been foolish to do so—but Cobbett was as critical of the *Report* and the political economists and 'Scotch feelosophers' behind it as he was of the Government. For Cobbett, resumption of gold payments had to be coupled with cancellation of interest payments on the national debt; otherwise, when prices fell, the burden of the debt would greatly increase. The common people would suffer worse than before, while the fundholders would be better off than ever.

Cobbett believed his 'Paper against Gold' to be the best of his life: he also thought of his currency views as being a kind of private hobby horse. Yet he was wrong in both these opinions. Vigorous as it was, 'Paper against Gold' was too dogmatic, and as for being unique in his interest in currency questions, Cobbett was merely one of many writers (and politicians) who, whether they liked to dwell on the issue or not or whether they understood it or not, were compelled to concern themselves with its intricacies. Currency and Corn, indeed, were to be the two main economic issues of the period between the end of the Napoleonic War and the burst of popular agitation that led to the passing of the Reform Bill in 1832. And the issues were all linked. The price of corn depended on the state of the currency as well as on the state of the harvest, and parliamentary reformers were sharply divided about what the right currency policy ought to be. When cash payments were resumed in 1819 by 'Peel's Act', some radicals, led by Cobbett, opposed the measure on the grounds that it was not accompanied by a cancellation of interest payments on the national debt, while others objected to dependence on gold and put their trust in mild inflationary pressure to keep incomes high and to reduce debt burdens.

In 1812, however, when Cobbett was eventually released from prison and returned in triumph to Botley, the country was thinking not so much about the value of money as about the problems of industry. The war itself had become seriously unpopular among many of the industrialists, particularly after February 1811, when the United States, in retaliation against British measures of economic warfare, as set out in successive Orders-in-Council, closed the American market to British goods. Middle-class agitation against the Orders-in-Council coincided with working-class agitation against machinery, and in the North and Midlands, in particular, Luddite disturbances seemed to threaten general social upheaval. Cobbett had no doubt where he himself stood. He opposed the Orders-in-Council and fully reported the machine-destroying riots, while attacking those newspapers and politicians who thought that riots could be suppressed by force and observing coolly that 'measures ought to be adopted, not so much for putting an end to riots, as to prevent the misery out of which they arise'. Indeed, he developed at this time a general view of the dynamics of popular disturbances which recent historians have 'discovered' as if it were new. The years of serious social tension were years when unemployment and high food prices coincided. You could not 'agitate a man' on a full stomach. 'The reasonings of the belly are always more powerful than those of the brain.'

It was during this crisis, when Cobbett interested himself more and more in the problems of *industrial* workers—and learned far more about them—that he changed his mind on the biggest question of all, the war. In a letter of 1812 he declared that the war had been fought not in the interests of the British people but of autocracy and corruption. 'The real cause of the war with France,' he concluded—and it was a complete *volte-face* from his position in 1801 and 1802—'was *the dread of a Parliamentary Reform in England.*' He no longer believed that it was possible to secure a complete victory over Napoleon, and failed to understand the significance of Napoleon's defeat in Spain or in Russia. He was even more worried about Britain's war with the United States, which began in 1812. He showed little enthusiasm at the fall of Napoleon in 1814 and still less when war was resumed with France after Napoleon's return from Elba. Even Waterloo did not fire him. His final summary of the war was couched in devastingly simple sentences:

> It added five hundred millions to the National Debt of England. It banished gold from circulation—It ruined commerce and manufactures in England; (in which) respect, it produced a new order of things both in Europe and America, both of which could then dispense with English goods. What inroads were made upon English liberty during this period, I need not attempt to describe, and, as to the weight of taxes, who needs to be told of that?

Not all these simple sentences were true, yet to Cobbett, who loved chains of connexions, they all hung together. They were, nonetheless, in sharp contrast with his earlier views. Although Cobbett's biographers seek to explain that there were fundamental consistencies beneath his changes of front, it is not easy to treat Cobbett's views on the war in 1813, 1814, and 1815 as developing naturally from his earlier prejudices. The truth was that he now thought that parliamentary reform was the only real issue that mattered. The war had become a diversion, and a dangerous diversion in that so long as it lasted it was all too easy to identify support for parliamentary reform with sedition or even treason. Once the war ended, 'to revile a man as a Jacobin will be senseless' and Reason—never before Cobbett's idol—would 'resume her sway'. 'The peace is, as I said it would be, a sort of *Revolution* in England.'

It was not. Rather the ending of the war added both to Britain's troubles and to the troubles of the ordinary people without bringing about reform. 'The play is over,' the pro-Government *Courier* had written when war ended, '*we may now go to supper.*' 'No,' Cobbett had to reply, '*you cannot yet go to supper.* You have not yet *paid for the play*. And before you have paid for the play, you will find that there is no money left for the supper.' The price to be paid was high. There was severe urban and rural unemployment as war business contracted and soldiers and sailors were demobilized, while the introduction of a corn law in 1815, seeking to protect English farmers by keeping out foreign corn except when the price of English corn was high, made matters worse rather than better for farm labourers without relieving anxiety among farmers. Everywhere there were signs of economic and social conflict. Yet the forces of Government, national and, more important, local, were far too strong to allow the situation to become genuinely revolutionary. Cobbett and his friends and allies who believed in parliamentary reform—Burdett, 'Orator' Hunt, Cochrane, and Major Cartwright, one of the oldest of the reformers with a record far longer than that of Cobbett—did their best to direct discontent into radical channels, but the very noise of their agitation produced as much panic and repression as conversion.

Cobbett was primarily concerned at first about 'agricultural distress,' but in 1815 and 1816 he began to appeal more and more to the 'journeymen and labourers', to whom he addressed a special message in November 1816 and for whom he produced a cheaper edition of the *Register* selling not for one shilling but for two-pence. His enemies called it 'twopenny trash', a name which he took up as enthusiastically as he had taken up the name 'Porcupine' in the Philadelphia of the 1790s. The circulation quickly rose to between 40,000 and 50,000 copies a week, and Cobbett obviously enjoyed, as he always had done, the exhilaration of what to him was genuine communication with his readers. As Edward Thompson has suggested in *The Making of the English Working Class*, 'Cobbett's thought was not a system but a relationship. Few writers can be found who were so much the "voice" of their own audience'. Avoiding abstractions, relying on homely metaphors, underlining the specific, above all exploiting personalities, as all popular journalists have subsequently been taught to do, Cobbett was able to achieve a unique impact.

By comparison, Burdett, who had very similar kinds of things to say, did not know instinctively quite how to say them. It is interesting to compare the verdict on the two men of Samuel Bamford, the young Lancashire working-class radical, whose reminiscences at their best have a freshness worthy of Cobbett himself.

At this time [after the war] [he observed] the writings of William Cobbett suddenly became of great authority: they were read on nearly every cottage hearth in the manufacturing districts of South Lancashire, in those of Leicester, Derby and Nottingham, also in many of the Scottish manufacturing towns. Their influence was speedily visible; he directed his readers to the true cause of their sufferings—misgovernment; and to its proper corrective; Parliamentary Reform. Riots soon became scarce, and from that time they never obtained their ancient vogue with the labourers of this country.

Yet of Burdett, one of his early heroes, whom he first met in 1817, on a deputation to London, Bamford wrote, 'his manner was dignified and civilly familiar; submitting to, rather than seeking conversation with men of our class'.

Cobbett himself claimed that he learned from his audience as well as enlightened it. 'It is the flint and steel meeting that brings forth the fire.' Certainly, in listing ten reasons for reform, Cobbett was trying to share with his readers the case for *controlled* agitation instead of sporadic upheaval and violence—an agitation with a definite set of objectives, the same set that the Chartists were to take up later in their famous 'Six Points'—destruction of the rotten boroughs; annual parliaments, the old radical cry of the eighteenth century; the ballot; no property qualifications for members of Parliament; equal electoral districts; and universal suffrage, to which he was converted by Major Cartwright, the link with the eighteenth century. Reform would end the mockery of corrupt elections, would abolish patronage, would reduce the costs of government, would lead to cuts in military and naval expenditure and save all secret service money spent on spies and informers, would reform the Bar (a matter on which Cobbett naturally had strong feelings), would restore the full freedom of the Press, and would stop interest payments on the swollen debt and thereby bring taxes down. By doing all these things, reform would *prevent* revolution and England's greatness would be restored.

The Government considered that all these things would constitute a revolution. 'Foul-mouthed' and 'blasphemous' were only two of the adjectives Cobbett's enemies used at this time. 'Why is it,' asked the *Quarterly Review*, the main Tory periodical, 'that this convicted incendiary is permitted week after week to sow the seeds of rebellion, insulting the Government and defying the laws of the country?' All his inconsistencies were pointed out, all his quirks of character. Cobbett knew that if the Government could pounce, it would. In March 1817 the Habeas Corpus Act was suspended and all 'agitators' at once became liable to imprisonment without trial. Further acts were also passed clamping down on radical meetings and publications. These measures were enough for Cobbett. 'A *dungeon,* or *silence* was my doom. I chose neither.' Once again, he decided abruptly to leave the country. Once again, the United States was his destination. On 17 April he sailed from Liverpool for New York. His wife stayed behind at Botley, but he took with him two of his sons.

6

AMERICAN INTERLUDE

COBBETT stayed in America until November 1819. He never
intended to emigrate, but he was out of England, therefore,
during two critical years, when radical forces were stirring everywhere and Government, local and national, was uncertain how
to handle them. Although he continued—in his inimitable way—
to receive English visitors and, by a supreme feat to edit the
Political Register from the United States, Cobbett lost much of
his direct influence over events during this period. His articles
had to deal with arguments rather than with news, or with the
kind of stale news that is anathema to the born journalist. His
reputation in consequence was not quite the same as it had been.
Nor did he avoid occasional absurdities of posture. He berated
Burdett, for example, for spending his time in Melton Mowbray
or in Brighton or in Ireland when he should have been in the
thick of the political battle, but there he was himself, thousands
of miles away in a farm on Long Island, devoting more of his
time to agriculture than to politics.

The quarrelsome side of Cobbett's disposition was frequently
on display during the American interlude, so that the kind of
radicalism he continued to advocate lost much of its unity and,
though the circumstances were favourable, some of its mo-
mentum. Cobbett was still out of England at the time of 'the
massacre of Peterloo' (August 1819), and was never quite able to
appreciate its full significance. When he arrived back, there were
many signs of economic, social, and political change, which it
took him time to assess. He failed, above all, to see that a radical
victory of any kind depended on a coalition of forces, that there
had to be a convergence of opinions and interests. In addition
to quarrelling with Burdett, who was certainly open to criticism,
he was drawn into more than one dispute with 'Orator' Hunt (he

44

had to lie his way out on one occasion) and the London radical tailor, Francis Place, who called him 'an impudent mountebank'. He was always contemptuous of the Whigs, even the reformers among them, and also bitterly and instinctively opposed to 'the antediluvian lawyer', Jeremy Bentham, the philosophical radical, who produced a far-reaching plan for parliamentary reform in 1819 which was to influence radicals and Whigs alike. For Cobbett 'the bombast' of Bentham's books was 'puzzling and tedious beyond mortal endurance' and he had made 'the idea of universal suffrage absurd by proposing to include women'. Bentham reciprocated by despising Cobbett. 'I contemplate Cobbett and Hunt,' he wrote, 'with much the same eye as the visitors of Mr. Carpenter, the optician (dealer in microscopes), contemplate the rabid animals devouring one another in a drop of water.' As a result of all these radical quarrels, Westminster was to become a showplace not of radical unity but of radical division between 1818 and 1830.

Far away in America, Cobbett revelled in a society which he found far more congenial than he had done in the 1790s—'a free country . . . and every labourer with plenty to eat and drink . . . and never to see the hang-dog face of a tax gatherer . . . no packed juries of tenants. . . . No hangings and rippings up. No Olivers. . . . No Cannings . . . Liverpools, Castlereaghs, Eldons, Ellenboroughs, or Sidmouths. . . . No Bankers. . . . No Wilberforces. Think of *that*!' On the positive side, Cobbett interested himself, above all, in American buildings, landscape, cultivation, and manners, producing one delightful book, *A Year's Residence in the United States*, which is a perfect companion piece to his later and more famous *Rural Rides* (1824). He also wrote a *Grammar of the English Language*, revised his earlier book *Le Tuteur Anglais,* and prepared a manual, *The American Gardener*, which was subsequently rewritten as *The English Gardener*.

G. D. H. Cole considered Cobbett's *Grammar* to be 'in some way his greatest work', combining grammatical rules with apt political examples. 'Sidmouth *writes* a Circular Letter; Sidmouth *wrote* a Circular Letter; Sidmouth will *write* a Circular Letter.'

'Among a select society of empty heads, "moderate reform" has long been a fashionable expression. How would they like to obtain *moderate justice* in a court of law, or to meet with moderate chastity in a wife?' *A Year's Residence* is an equally remarkable *tour de force*. Few books about America have a more sturdy and intimate sense of place. Few books can turn vegetables into such remarkable objects of controversy. Potatoes ('Irish Potatoes') are roundly denounced, as vehemently as Wilberforce: they are 'a root worse than useless', a dangerous staple food permitting degradation of living standards. By contrast the Swedish turnip is a superb feeding stuff, and American corn is a perfect export. Interspersed with lyrical accounts of 'fowls fattening, ducks coming along to meet the green peas, chickens ready for the asparagus' and the merits of beer, unappreciated in America, there are lampoons both of Shakespeare and of Milton and re-markable political allusions, which reveal that Cobbett's imagination as well as his intellect still brooded over what was happening back home. He was disappointed, for example, with the birds. 'Here are, indeed, birds which bear the *name* of robin, blackbird, thrush and goldfinch; but alas! the thing at Westminster has, in the manner, the *name* of Parliament, and speaks the voice of the people, whom it pretends to represent, in much about the same degree that the blackbird here speaks the voice of its namesake in England.'

One night in May 1819 Cobbett's house was burnt down. As soon as possible he returned to England. The most remarkable aspect of his journey back was that he took with him the bones of Tom Paine which, since Paine was an atheist, had been buried in unhallowed ground on his farm. Paine obviously haunted Cobbett. He was now treated as 'a truly great man' before whose 'expiring flambeau' Cobbett wanted to light his taper. Cobbett also wanted to write a new life of Paine. There was a kind of basic symbolism in Cobbett's gesture that brings out neglected sides of his personality. He was interested in religious questions, but never drawn to atheism as Paine was, and Paine's body was now as precious to him as the bones of any saint.

46

7

THE RADICAL IN ACTION

It was not only Cobbett who dealt in symbols in 1819. Once 'Peterloo' had subsided, interest in English radical politics shifted from the misfortunes of the poor to the misfortunes of Queen Caroline, the wife whom George IV persistently refused to recognize. On coming to the throne in 1820 after eight years of regency, George IV was anxious that Caroline, whom he viewed as his 'greatest enemy', should neither be crowned nor treated in any other respect as Queen. Despite her unsavoury character, the radicals immediately took up her cause and made the very most of the unprecedented unpopularity of the King. The colourful private lives of both George and Caroline became matters of general public discussion, and there was an element of sordid melodrama, tinged with genuine pathos, in the unfolding of events. Until her death in August 1821, Caroline was a radical symbol, particularly in turbulent London, the idol of the crowds and a constant embarrassment to the Government.

Cobbett, for all his professional belief in monarchy, which he never abandoned, was one of the most zealous advocates of her cause. She was just about as different from his ideal of womanhood—neat, modest, obedient womanhood—as any woman could be, yet he wrote speeches and letters for her—including one letter of remonstrance to the King, the authorship of which for a time he disclaimed—received working-class deputations on her behalf, and devoted almost every page of the *Political Register* to her cause. He was even prepared to tolerate addresses from 'female reformers', whom he normally despised. It is true that he maintained, perhaps a little too vehemently, that he always regarded 'the affair of the queen as an *incident* in the Great Drama, of which the working of the Funds, or Debt, is a plot; a *great*

47

incident, indeed, but still an incident'. 'A knock on the head may help out of the world a man perishing from cancer' was another of his homely metaphors. Yet he made too much of the incident, and it was not '*the* knock on the head'.

Before the beginning of the Queen Caroline affair, Cobbett had already tried to resume political activities where he had left them off. He campaigned, for example, as a radical candidate for Coventry, where he took part in March 1820 in a rough election, in which he polled only 517 votes. Life was not easy for him, however, since the notorious 'Six Acts' passed by the Government in the wake of Peterloo further muzzled the Press, restricted the right of public meetings, and increased the power of the local magistrates. The sixth act subjected 'certain publications' to the newspaper tax. *Twopenny trash* henceforth had a tax of four-pence added to it. Circulation naturally fell sharply, and an effort by Cobbett to start a new daily evening paper *The Evening Post* failed totally. A fighting fund to help his campaign at Coventry and that of other radical candidates, *Cobbett's Fund for Reform*, was also quickly dissipated. As a result, Cobbett, who like many other writers on public finance was never entirely able to manage his own, went bankrupt in 1820. His creditors, particularly Burdett, to whom he acknowledged no gratitude, treated him generously, but he had to sell his house and estate near Botley and rent a property at Brompton. The combined capital of his family at this time was three shillings in silver and a few coppers, and only a loan of twenty pounds kept the *Political Register* alive.

The year 1820, therefore, had been one of the most difficult in Cobbett's life. Indeed, three libel cases, one brought by John Wright and two by a fellow reformer Thomas Cleary, all three the result of Cobbett's own truculence, added to the drama of bankruptcy. Cobbett remained enviably confident in the middle of the distress. There was little introspection. 'Gentleman,' he told his friends, 'you will see that this, like every other "sinking" that I have experienced, will be at last a *mounting* in place of a sinking.' He was right. The loss of Botley freed him of a com-mitment, the cost of which he had found it difficult to measure.

Wright troubled him no more. He could remould his private life. In 1821 he was to move from Brompton to Kennington to 'four acres of rich land for cows and pigs, surrounded by nursery gardens'. It would be 'quite enough for Papa's amusement', his daughter Anne wrote percipiently, 'though not sufficient to drag him into any great expenses'.

Cobbett's most important work in the 1820s was literary, although there was never any danger that he would leave politics out. He enriched his vocabulary of vituperation during this period by adding Malthus, the distinguished writer on population, to the special short list which was still headed by Wilberforce. 'Parson Malthus' wanted to keep population down. Cobbett's reply was, 'keep out': he had already written to Malthus from America in 1819 telling him simply: 'I have, during my life, detested many men but never any one so much as you.' Cobbett had his own stubborn views on population, as he had on education—and his educational views hardened also in the 1820s in face of the new Society for the Diffusion of Useful Knowledge—but in the former case the views were plainly erroneous. He did not believe that the English population was increasing, and no Census could ever prove to him that it was.

On three particular political issues he had, as usual, an important and distinctive contribution to make. First, he succeeded where no other early nineteenth-century radical ever succeeded, in winning substantial support for a radical programme in the rural areas. In 1821 he issued in the *Register* what he called a special *New Year's Gift to Farmers* and even made an appeal to landlords too. These and other writings were collected in a pamphlet, *The Farmer's Friend* (1822), followed up by the *Farmer's Wife's Friend*. There was enough agricultural discontent at this time for Cobbett to make the most of the 'criminal' return to gold on the wrong terms by Peel's Act of 1819. He had promised in 1819 itself that if he were wrong about his gloomy predictions he would give Castlereagh leave 'to put me on a gridiron and broil me alive, while Sidmouth stirs the fire, and Canning stands by making a jest of my groans'. The offer still stood after the suicide of Castlereagh in 1822 and the resignation of Sidmouth from the Cabinet in 1824, and a representation of the gridiron frequently appeared at the head of the *Political Register*. Farmers obviously liked the non-abstract appeal of the most abstract subject of all, the currency. They were suffering heavily from debt burdens contracted during the wars, from high taxation and the mounting poor rate, and they approved of the blend of advice and attack in Cobbett's writings. Many of them were electors under the unreformed parliamentary system, and they felt, like he, that they could get little out of either 'orthodox' Whigs or Tories.

Against this background, Cobbett had a remarkable success in January 1823 in getting a duly summoned county meeting of electors in Norfolk—which recalled the great county reform meetings of the early 1780s—to agree on a petition asking for the application of Church property and income raised from sale of Crown Lands to the liquidation of the national debt; what he called 'an equitable adjustment of the debt', in other words a repudiation of interest on the national debt; a reduction of the standing army; and a total abolition of sinecures and pensions. He also produced a *Norfolk Yeoman's Gazette* to try to extend his campaign. The campaign soon failed, however. Times improved, large farmers disapproved of his views on enclosure, and it was impossible to maintain any continuous organization. Although there was a severe currency crisis in 1825—coupled with a more general economic crisis—and a year of prosperity was succeeded by mounting 'distress', Cobbett did not gain immediately or directly in support. He did have the dubious satisfaction, none the less, of holding his long deferred 'Feast of the Gridiron' to celebrate the coming true of the predictions which he had made in 1819: the principal toast was to 'the industrious and labouring people: May their raiment cease to be taken from them by the juggling of the paper money system'.

The second political issue with which Cobbett was concerned was industrial. Paradoxically, the Queen Caroline affair had diverted his attention to conditions in the new factories and to the existence of trade unions. Throughout the 1820s he gave his blessing to trade unions, showing little sympathy, however, for strikes, which seemed to him to dissipate working-class energies. He supported the legalization of trade unions in 1824 and gave something of a lead in demanding factory legislation to control factory conditions. When in 1824 a proposal was made to erect a statue in Manchester to James Watt, 'the great steam engine projector', Cobbett wrote a most powerful article *Cotton Lords and What's Watt* asking cotton lords in effect to keep their own mills in order. He wrote freely at this time of 'the working classes of the community', still a new phrase, and poured scorn on the older phrase 'lower orders': the one was an insider's phrase, the other a patronising, often insolent, outsider's view of other people. Yet Cobbett himself never thought consecutively or consistently in class terms and objected to anyone who behaved in such a way that he 'cut off the chains of connexion between rich and poor'. He still believed in the old society, not in the new. After fighting and losing the election of 1826 at Preston in Lancashire—with the help of an East Anglian squire, Sir Thomas Beevors, whom he had rallied to his side in Norfolk—he produced a new work, *The Poor Man's Friend*, in which he re-stated his old views in a new setting. 'Bare bones and rags are the true marks of the real slave. What is the object of government? To cause men to live happily?' *The Poor Man's Friend* was Cobbett's own favourite work: it had as its sub-title 'A Defence of the Rights of those who do the Work and fight the Battles'.

The third political issue in which Cobbett became interested—Catholic Emancipation—was directly relevant in Preston, where there was an exceptionally large number of Catholic voters. Cobbett was a vigorous advocate of Catholic Emancipation in the mid-20s, although he quarrelled fiercely with Daniel O'Connell, who was its unchallenged champion, about religious politics in Ireland and the extent of the Irish franchise. He was more consistent on both these issues than O'Connell, but he was also jealous of the popular appeal O'Connell—'Big O', he called him—

could make. Cobbett's own contribution to Catholic Emancipation was made as much through his remarkable *History of the Protestant Reformation*, which appeared in numbers in 1824 and 1825, as through political agitation. In this polemical survey, which rested on a basis of historical fact drawn from the Catholic John Lingard's *History of England* (1819), Cobbett not only revealed English bigotry and Catholic oppression, but traced back all the problems of his country to the Reformation. The Reformation, indeed, was seen as the origin of 'The Thing', the connected system of privilege and corruption which he had always been fighting. This book is important not only because of the huge circulation it achieved, but because of the light it throws on Cobbett. Never did he display more dazzlingly his ability to find connexions and to uncover mysteries. His theory of rights was essentially historical, while Paine's had been theoretical and deductive. Now Cobbett's sense of history was enriched and, as far as he was concerned, the case was clinched. He did not want to become a Catholic, but he wanted everyone to see why Catholics were what they were. He also gazed back into the Middle Ages, when there was neither poor law nor pauperism: many others were to gaze there too, contrasting past and present, as the 'age of improvement' continued farther into the nineteenth century.

Among his writings, *Rural Rides* is now much the best known. In 1821 Cobbett began to write the famous accounts of his journeys on horseback: they were later published in book form in 1830, and they still stand out as the best record of a lost but not forgotten England, combining, as they do, vivid detail and bold generalization. They are not a 'nature book', yet they contain memorable descriptions both of landscape and villages and towns. The digressions about the formation of clouds, the pretty faces of the local girls, or the history of the parish churches can be as interesting to the reader as the 'interconnections' Cobbett loved to trace between people, places, and events. Yet, above all, Cobbett as always, revealed himself at the centre of things, deliberately avoiding the new turnpike roads for example or picking out the 'villainous rotten boroughs', or just musing on his 'life of adventure, of toil, of peril, of pleasure, of ardent friendship and not less ardent enmity' and wondering why 'a heart and mind so wrapped up in everything belonging to the gardens, the fields and the woods should have been condemned to waste themselves away amidst the stench, the noise and the strife of cities'.

Two other of his books should not be left unread. His *Advice to Young Men* (1829) has less about politics in it than most of his books and explains why Cobbett could be treated not only as a hero of self-help but as 'the pattern John Bull of his century'. 'It is the duty, and ought to be the pleasure, of age and experience,' he writes, 'to warn and instruct youth'; and, somewhat pompous though the thought may seem to be, there was nothing pompous about the book. Like anything else Cobbett wrote, it is on occasion crotchety as well as independent, and for all its healthy and robust practical wisdom, it shows the limits of a mind never prepared to examine searchingly the origins of prejudice or the variety of opinions. There was much in other people's experience which Cobbett was doomed never to understand. His *Sermons* (1822) are even more remarkable in their intensely direct and independent style and content, satirizing the 'moral tracts' which were issued in their thousands by Hannah More ('the old Bishop in Petticoats') and the Evangelicals. For an understanding of Cobbett's own morality they are indispensable, with the titles of such sermons as 'Bribery', 'Unjust Judges', 'The Sluggard', and 'Forbidding Marriage' (savagely anti-Malthusian) giving a good clue to the nature of the message. These were the sermons which were *not* preached from the pulpits of the day.

Cobbett used to advertise the 'library' of books he had written. 'When I am asked,' he began the advertisement, 'what books a young man or young woman ought to read, I always answer, let him or her read *all the books that I have written*. This does, it will doubtless be said, *smell of the shop*. It is what I recommended.' As always, however, the egotism has to be related to other parts of the advertisement. Absurd though the final statement in the advertisement was that 'here is a stock of knowledge sufficient for any young man, in the world'—how he would have satirized anybody else who made such a claim—the advertisement as printed in 1830 also included the sentence 'in about everyone of these works I have pleaded the cause of the *working people* and I shall now see that cause triumph in spite of all that can be done to prevent it'. Cobbett wanted a system which would allow others to be as independent as himself. In *Rural Rides* also he had written in 1825 of 'events working together to make the country worth living in, which, for the great body of people, is at present hardly the case'.

Cobbett was more right about 1830 than about 1825, but for the wrong reasons. It was not so much the very real re-animation of radical activity in 1829 or 1830 which made for an effective convergence of reform politics in 1830 as the divisions among the Tories, the death of George IV, and the return of the Whigs to power. The Whigs were determined to introduce a measure of parliamentary reform. It was bound to be more restricted in scope than the radical reform demanded by Cobbett and his friends, yet it proved sufficiently far-reaching to alarm their Tory opponents in Parliament. The Whig view, sincerely held, that the Reform Bill was necessary if revolution was to be avoided was countered by the Tory argument that the Reform Bill in itself constituted a revolution. This was a deep political difference, even though both sides shared the same views about the rights of property, the cohesion of the social system, and the need to preserve the constitution.

Preoccupied as he was with his own campaigns, Cobbett did not fully understand all this, and his failure to do so hampered him in the critical years from 1830 to 1832 as far as the issue of parliamentary reform—*his* issue as he had always seen it—was concerned. On the one hand, he was not at the centre of the political stage, and other radical leaders, notably Thomas Attwood, leader of the Birmingham Political Union, played a more important role in relation to the quadrilateral of political forces—Whig Government, Tory opposition (entrenched in the House of Lords), King, and public opinion. On the other hand, he did not criticize the limitations of the Whig Bill as did 'Orator' Hunt and the leaders of the newly-founded National Union of the Working Classes (1831) with their powerful journal *The Poor Man's Guardian*. Unable to admire the Whigs, Cobbett was thus at the same time out of tune with their extreme radical opponents, and particularly so when they turned towards republicanism. They wanted to make things new: he still wished to return to the old. When in 1830 Hunt won an election at Preston, where Cobbett had failed, Cobbett was soon dismissing him viciously as 'the Preston cock on the Preston dunghill'. This abuse did not mean that Cobbett thought much either of the London radicals, particularly Francis Place, who backed the Whig bill. He had little part to play in the important radical debates in London between 'popular radicals' and 'philosophical radicals' concerning the best way to support the Whigs in their fight to get the bill through. Indeed Cobbett, who himself believed the bill would begin a new era, was completely out of touch with the people who mattered.

He remained in touch, however, with many of the people 'who did not matter', particularly through the medium of his revived *Twopenny Trash* (1830) and through the meetings he addressed in Manchester or in Birmingham (where he debated currency policy for two days with Attwood). Above all, he knew how to talk to country folk, not so much about parliamentary reform as about agricultural distress—the big social issue which meant more to Cobbett when the crisis came than all the political items in the radical programme. 'A rebellion of the belly' among the village labourers spread through the countryside in the autumn of 1830. There was burning of ricks and barns and an 'epidemic' (for such was the word generally used) of machine breaking. Cobbett sympathized, as always, with the rural poor and condemned the Whig Government as fiercely as he had condemned any of its predecessors for seeking to put down the 'revolt' by counter-violence. He expressed himself glad that despite 'all the palaver in the world, all the wheedling, coaxing and praying . . . all the teaching of the Tract Societies, all the imprisoning, whipping and harnessing to carts and waggons', the 'honest, industrious English labourer' was still fighting to show that he had 'an indefeasible right to live'. This right, in the last resort, mattered to Cobbett more than the ballot or even the suffrage, on both of which issues he was prepared to change his mind in 1831 and 1832. For arguing that 'out of evil comes good'—wages were being raised and tithes reduced—and for claiming that nothing happened in the countryside 'until the labourers revolt', Cobbett was attacked by Whigs and Tories alike (and even by some radicals). When one Sussex labourer under sentence of death for firing a hayrick 'confessed' that he should never have thought of doing such a thing 'if Mr. Cobet had never given aney lactures', Cobbett was charged with publishing a libel with intent to incite labourers to acts of violence and was brought to trial in July 1831.

This time, in the last trial of his life, the jury failed to agree. Cobbett conducted his own defence by moving straight on to the attack and putting the Government into the dock instead of himself. He even produced a letter from Henry Brougham, the Whig Lord Chancellor, asking one of Cobbett's sons to allow the Government to use an old article of his published in 1816 in order to calm down the Luddite machine breakers. 'Whatever may be the verdict of the jury,' he ended, 'if I am doomed to spend my last breath in a dungeon, I will pray God to bless my country; I will curse the Whigs and leave my revenge to my children and the labourers of England.' After the jury had failed to agree, the Government dropped the case. Instead of going to a dungeon Cobbett—at the age of 69—was elected a member of Parliament in December 1832 in the first general election under the reformed system.

8

MEMBER OF PARLIAMENT

Cobbett spent three years sitting in the House of Commons, what he had always referred to ironically as 'the Collective Wisdom'. His constituency, a new one, was industrial not rural, Northern not Southern—the smoky industrial mill town of Oldham, on one side of Manchester, where Cobbett had also been nominated as a candidate and had won a considerable number of Tory second votes. His fellow-member for Oldham, John Fielden, owned one of the largest cotton mills in the country, but shared most of Cobbett's views about the rights of the poor and the need to humanize industry and to reform agriculture. Both men were returned by a large majority. 'A FARMER I WILL LIVE AND DIE', Cobbett had proclaimed in capital letters in June 1832: 'now I belong to the people of Oldham,' he added six months later.

Certainly he took his new duties very seriously, although he soon found that the parliamentary timetable was so organized as to reverse the careful habits of a lifetime. It seemed absurd to him, for instance, to stay up late instead of getting up early. His very first words in Parliament affectively registered his mood. 'It seems to me that since I have been sitting here I have heard a great deal of unprofitable discussion.' Despite the Reform Act, the old Parliament was not significantly different in composition or tone from its pre-reform counterpart, and the small group of radical members was divided and leaderless. Cobbett himself was one of the few 'curiosities', but he was no more capable of leading a radical group than he was of adjusting himself to unfamiliar and uncongenial parliamentary procedures, and when as one of his first acts he moved that the King be requested to erase Peel's name from his list of Privy Councillors because of his Currency Act of 1819 his symbolic gesture was received with marked hostility and his motion defeated by 298 votes to 6. In October 1834, when part of the Houses of Parliament was burned down, Cobbett suggested simply that the agency was 'fire and brimstone from Heaven'. None the less, he was re-elected to Parliament in 1835, and he spoke so often and introduced so many proposals that a fellow satirist wrote a sonnet beginning:

> *Mr. Cobbett asked leave to bring in very soon*
> *A Bill to abolish the sun and the moon.*

Cobbett made one superb speech in Parliament—on the Factory Bill of 1833—and took a major share in the opposition to the most important piece of legislation of the period, the new Poor Law of 1834. His speech on factories was superb, because it was quite exceptionally terse and economical. Attacking those who refused to legislate to control the hours of child labour in the factories on the grounds that the country could not afford to interfere, Cobbett taunted the reformed Commons with having made a great discovery—that 'the shipping, the land, and the Bank and its credit, are all worth nothing compared with the labour of three hundred thousand little girls in Lancashire'. His fight against the poor law was protracted and unsuccessful, yet it was the right kind of cause to fire both his imagination and his energy. Supported by most Whigs and Tories alike, the Bill of 1834 abolished outdoor relief, deliberately set out to make conditions in the workhouses less acceptable than the worst conditions outside, broke up families by separately treating the individual poor, husbands, wives, and children, and created a new administrative system based not on the parish but on a central Poor Law Commission and elected boards of guardians. Every aspect of the act was anathema to Cobbett: it was, indeed, the complete anti-Cobbett measure, denying, so it seemed to him, the inalienable rights of the poor while establishing the worst possible kind of centralized bureaucratic organization to make the new system 'work'. When it passed, Cobbett predicted 'a dreadful convulsion'. Already disillusioned by the Reform Bill, he treated the new poor law as a 'great and terrible innovation'. The only satisfaction he got out of it all was that a few genuine Tories agreed with him on this issue.

Cobbett continued to publish the *Political Register* until his death and—for a time—his son continued it after him. He could not bring himself to cut himself off from his public, although he was often tempted to do so. Trade unionism interested him also, and so did Ireland, where he paid a last visit in the autumn of 1834. He had plans for writing a book on Ireland when he died, as he had plans for publishing his own autobiography. He also wrote a series of trenchant *Legacies*—to Peel, to Labourers, and to Parsons. He enjoyed his last years with his wife and family on his leased farm, Normandy Farm, not far from Farnham, but there were family troubles and in any case he could never return to a state of rural innocence like that of his boyhood. 'The whole fabric of the ancient government' seemed to be 'falling to pieces'. 'Monopolists and usurers were living in luxury': the new railways were 'unnatural effects', signs that the resources of the nation had been 'drawn unnaturally together into great heaps'. On the surface more Tory than radical—so, too, as always, at the core—Cobbett was independent and truculent to the end:

> Some generations, at least, will pass away before the name of William Cobbett will cease to be familiar in the mouths of the people of England, and for the rest of the world I care not a straw.

The final entry in his diary (for 12 June) read, 'Ploughing home field.'

He died on 18 June 1835 and was buried—in pouring rain—in Farnham churchyard. Miles away in smoky Manchester, the *Advertiser* wrote 'with the deepest regret' that 'the labourers of England have lost the very best friend they ever had. Peace to his ashes.'

PRINCIPAL DATES

1763   Born at Farnham, Surrey.
1783–4   Worked as a lawyer's clerk in London.
1784–91   Served in the Army, reaching the rank of Serjeant-Major.
1792   Married Ann Reid.
1792–3   Lived in France.
1793–1800 Lived in the United States.
1800   Returned to England.
1802   Started the *Political Register*.
1805   Acquired his farm at Botley.
1810   Trial and imprisonment in Newgate.
1816   Started cheap *Register*.
1817   Fled to America.
1819   Returned from America with Paine's bones.
1826   Unsuccessfully fought Preston election.
1830   Began *Twopenny Trash*.
1832   Elected Member of Parliament for Oldham.
1835   Re-elected. Death.

FOR FURTHER READING

THE fullest life of Cobbett is G. D. H. Cole, *The Life of William Cobbett* (3rd edn. Horne and Van Thal, 1947). Perhaps the best introduction to Cobbett, however, is the cleverly knit together collection of his autobiographical fragments edited by W. Reitzel and called in its 1947 edition *The Autobiography of William Cobbett, the Progress of a Plough-Boy to a Seat in Parliament*, (Faber). There is a shorter Penguin autobiography by W. Baring Pemberton, *William Cobbett* (1949), and a brilliantly written little book by G. K. Chesterton, *William Cobbett* (Hodder and Stoughton, 1926). On Cobbett's American career M. E. Clark's *Peter Porcupine in America* (University of Pennsylvania, 1939) is indispensable. There is a full bibliographical study of Cobbett's writings by M. L. Pearl, *William Cobbett, A Bibliographical Account of His Life and Times* (Oxford, 1953). Among Cobbett's own available writings, his *Papers Against Gold* (first published 1815), his *Advice to Young Men* (first published, 1829), his *Rural Rides* (first published, 1830; Everyman edn., Dent, 1956), and his *Twopenny Trash* (first published, 1831), are most easily and generally accessible. All should be read. Only the *Political Register* (1802–25), however, gives the reader the fullest sense of Cobbett's gifts, interest, range and style.

INDEX